FUEL THE

FIRE

BLAZE Through Life!

Stay motivated
and live a life of
purpose, passion and power.

JOHN ARBOLEDA

Published by John Arboleda

Copyright © 2015

Printed in the United States of America

Arboleda, John
     Fuel the Fire, Blaze Through Life: Stay motivated and live a life of purpose, passion and power

ISBN: 978-0-578-15877-8

Warning —Disclaimer
The purpose of this book is to educate and entertain. The author or publisher does not guarantee that anyone following the techniques, suggestions, tips, ideas, or strategies will become successful. The author and publisher shall have neither liability or responsibility to anyone with respect to loss or damage caused, or alleged to be caused, directly or indirectly by information contained in this book.

"If you're ready to **achieve more success and happiness,** then read and absorb the strategies in this book by John Arboleda!"

—**James Malinchak,** Featured on
ABC's Hit TV Show, *Secret Millionaire,*
Best-selling Co-Author of *Chicken Soup for the College Soul,*
The World's #1 Big Money Speaker® Trainer & Coach
Founder, www.BigMoneySpeaker.com

"John Arboleda has written this generations *Who Moved My Cheese.*
**We all WANT to stay motivated, but we lack a road map.
NOT ANYMORE.** Thank you John."

—**Alicia Taylor,** *Oprah Winfrey Network*
Finalist for *Your Own Show*

"John masterfully explains the principles of motivation. **His philosophy can enhance the quality of life for anyone** who embraces it. Bottom line, this book ROCKS!"

—**Craig Duswalt,** Speaker, author, radio host and
creator of the *RockStar System for Success,*
www.craigduswalt.com

"A brilliant book told in a fun and unique way! *Fuel the Fire* guides the reader down the path of success in business and in life with a moral compass."

—**Glenn Pardon,** Entrepreneur,
executive sales coach

"John has created an **extraordinary blueprint for human potential, business growth, and life** by revealing the philosophy behind his own personal success and the reasons why it can work for anyone. Truly Magical!"

—**John Formica,** *Ex-Disney Guy,*
America's Customer Experience Coach

"A must read that **will empower you** to discover your innermost desires."

—**Jill Lublin,** International speaker and
3x's best selling author, including *Guerrilla Publicity,*
Publicity Crash Course.com

I dedicate this book to my amazing mom and dad, whom I lovingly refer to as "mami y papi".

Thank you for all of the love, happiness and strength you have shared with my brothers and me throughout our entire lives.

Los quiero mucho!

CONTENTS

Author's Opening Thoughts

We all pursue a few specific things in life to find happiness and fulfillment. Success at work, rewarding personal and professional relationships, stress free lives, a bountiful supply of money in the bank, freedom to explore the world, and health that will grant us the energy and longevity to enjoy all that we are blessed with.

If you ask people what they need or want, to find fulfillment in their lives, many will be able to have a lengthy conversation giving you all the details of their master plan.

Then when you most likely follow up with the question of how they are putting their plan into action, the conversation converts to a list of reasons why "action" has not or will not occur.

The question then arises, "If we know what we need and want to find ultimate success in life, why don't we routinely implement the activities in our lives to make our dreams a reality?"

The good news is that this book will give you the solution. It will show you how to stay motivated to help you implement your daily activities.

Another question that arises is, "Why does our motivation to pursue the life that we vibrantly plan, fizzle away?"

The answer to this question, along with the solution, is the inspiration for this book.

INTRODUCTION

This story will show you 5 proven strategies that will help you stay motivated. It is a reality that staying motivated is not easy. This is why you need to have a plan to keep yourself motivated, and that is exactly what this book will give you. If the scenario that follows resembles your life in any way, you have nothing to worry about; your guide for success is just a few pages away.

Have you been motivated by different events at various times in your life? You read a book or a quote, watched a movie, talked to a friend or even a stranger, listened to a song, connected with a picture, had a life changing moment, set a New Year's resolution, or went to a motivational seminar, and....

"You were inspired!"

This inspiration ignites ideas. It evokes positive feelings, and colorful images that run through your mind. You become motivated to make a positive change in your life.

"Inspiration is the spark, which ignites your motivation, which will help you blaze through life."
John Arboleda

A burst of energy runs through your veins and you create a plan. You imagine, someday soon, celebrating the accomplishment of your goals. The very next day you excitedly and anxiously put the plan into action, with every intention of following the plan until you succeed.

Then what happens?

Days pass and the excitement to continue on your new journey starts to dissipate. It slowly fades like fog in the late morning.

You find reasons to slowdown progress on your new plan.

"I am too busy at work."

"The kids take all of my time."

"I am exhausted when I get home after a long day."

Slowly, day by day, you fall back into your old pattern. The images in your mind that once filled you with joy at the thought of accomplishing your new goals become distant.

The emotions that jolted you to make positive changes in your life slowly disappear.

As a result, the life changes you envisioned and wildly craved are now in hiatus, once again.

Eventually, your plan for success and your newfound goals are no longer a priority in your life.

This will result in you reverting to the activities and habits that have defined your life. The same life you desire to change. Life goes on.

Days pass and turn into weeks. Weeks become months. Months blend into years and your life passes you by. Your stark reality will be that you have made little progress, no progress, or your situation has taken a turn for the worse.

The obvious question is, "How can you keep yourself motivated to avoid this from happening to you over and over again in your life?"

The answer.....

You need to have a plan to keep yourself motivated that will keep you connected to your goals.

The question that follows is, "Why does your motivation disappear almost as quickly as it once sparked to life?"

The answer.....

It is because you are not consistently fueling the internal fire that keeps your motivation alive.

This story will show you 5 proven strategies you can use to fuel your internal fire to stay motivated.

Incorporate into your life the activities I share throughout this book and you will live a life of purpose, passion, and power!

THE EPIPHANY

"The only person you are destined to become is the person you decide to be.

–Ralph Waldo Emerson

The sun was shining brightly on a beautiful summer morning. Flowers extended their petals to catch every ray of sun that beamed down from above and a breeze made the trees dance.

It was on this morning that Jacob, a young executive, was walking by the lake near his home. He was deep in thought reflecting on his personal and professional life.

Earlier in the day he reviewed the goals that he had written at the beginning of the year. He was distraught. He had accomplished or was on track to only accomplishing a couple of the goals that he had set for himself.

He was off course and he was puzzled. Why had he strayed from his initial plan?

He had prepared so well.

He had goals and had even written them down. Each goal was precise and was accompanied by actionable targets. He had a timeline associated with each goal; he set goals for his career, and his personal life to create a balance.

He could recall the excitement and energy he felt when he wrote his goals at the beginning of the year. He remembered how focused and motivated he was as he started putting his plan into action.

Accomplishing his goals was a top priority for him.

"What happened?" He asked himself.

As he strolled by the calm waters of the lake, he looked deep within himself to find the answer and he had an epiphany.

"My motivation lost its flurry day after day. Then, as my passion dwindled, I lost focus."

This was the reason he did not make consistent progress towards achieving his goals. He realized that he needed to find a way to stay motivated throughout the year. If he did not, his path to success would be tainted with constant disappointments.

Jacob had a friend who had achieved tremendous success over the years in his personal and professional life. His friend's name was Mr. Wiseman, who we will refer to as Mr. W. He knew that Mr. W. would be able to give him the answers that he needed.

Fuel the Fire...Blaze Through Life

"THE WHY..."

"The two most important days in your life are the day you are born and the day you find out why."

–Mark Twain

Jacob barely slept due to the excitement.

He knew if he learned proven strategies to stay motivated, he would succeed far more often than he would fail. Each victory would mean being one step closer to his goals.

Early Monday morning, Jacob called Mr. W.

Jacob explained his epiphany, and asked for a meeting.

Mr. W responded, "If you have an appetite for learning, let's feed it!"

Mr. W. could feel Jacob's excitement over the phone and he graciously invited Jacob to his home that afternoon.

Jacob arrived 10 minutes early to Mr. W's home. He knew Mr. W. did not appreciate it if you arrived late or too early.

Mr. W. welcomed Jacob with a great big hug and a sincere smile. They went to the backyard and sat by the pool.

"How can I help you?", asked Mr. W.

"I would like to learn your secrets to staying motivated. I become inspired; write down my goals, start working towards them but then my motivation slowly fades away. Then, I end up right where I started after a few months. What can I do to keep myself motivated?"

"That is a great question. It is one that I asked my mentor many years ago. What I learned changed my life and what you will learn will undoubtedly change yours as well", replied Mr. W.

"Great, thank you Mr. W!" Jacob replied.

Jacob excitedly opened up his bag, took out 4 new notepads, and took the cap off his pen. He had a smile from ear to ear and he said, "I know there is probably a lot that I need to learn, but I'm ready when you are Mr. W."

Mr. W. gently chuckled and replied.

"I love your spirit. You will need to focus on five different areas. I will discuss the first one with you. Then, I will send you to three other people to learn about the three other strategies. Finally, we will meet once again to talk about the last topic. The people you will meet successfully implement all five strategies, but they are exceptional in the area that they will talk to you about."

Mr. W. proceeded to instruct Jacob in the first lesson.

"Let me tell you a story about my dad. When he was a young father in his early thirties; he worked two full time jobs. He worked from 7am-4pm at his first job and from 5pm-2am at his second job. He made enough money at his first job to pay for his home, basic bills and for his family to live a modest life. The reason he continued to sacrifice and work at the second job was because he wanted to have his 3 kids study in a private school. His dream was to send his kids to college. He believed a great education would give his kids every opportunity to succeed in life.

He worked 16 hour days and slept in the back of his pick-up truck, several days a week, because he was too exhausted to drive home. This was his routine, day in and day out, for 5 years. Amazingly, he always had a smile on his face."

Mr. W. paused for a couple of seconds.

Mr. W. continued, "He woke up many days exhausted and did not want to go to work, but he did. Many times he thought about quitting the second job, but he didn't. There were many naysayers telling him he was working too much and that he was crazy. He ignored their negative comments and kept away from these people to stay focused on his goals."

This story had a special place in Mr. W.'s heart. As he reminisced, he quietly sat back in his chair, smiled, closed his eyes for a couple of seconds, crossed his fingers behind his neck, and took a deep breath.

When he opened his eyes, Jacob could see the tears of appreciation that built up above his eye lids, but the tears did not overflow onto his cheeks. Mr. W. was reflecting on the sacrifice his father made for the well being of his mother and siblings.

Mr. W. continued.

"What kept my father motivated? The "why" behind his goal. Once you have clearly determined the "why" behind the goals you set, it anchors your motivation to keep it from drifting away.

"Once you have clearly determined the "why" behind the goals that you set, it anchors your motivation to keep it from drifting away."

The "why" will keep your motivation alive, which will compel you to pursue your goals regardless of the challenges you will face. He had a very clear reason why he was sacrificing the way he was. It wasn't for the money or to live in a glamorous home. He wanted to provide a safe home for his family, while at the same time setting his kids up for a brighter future with a top notch education. Jacob, every goal that you set has to have a clear and defined "why" in order for you to sustain the motivation you need to accomplish it.

This was a new perspective for Jacob. When he wrote his goals he knew what he wanted to accomplish but he did not clearly define "why" he wanted to accomplish each goal.

Jacob replied, "I now understand how "why" will keep me motivated. If the reason for me to accomplish my goal is clearly defined, it will fuel my motivation to keep me on course. The "why" will instill within me the foundation to sustain the pursuit for the life that I want to have, or that I want to provide for others. When I am weary, frustrated, faced with unforeseen challenges or surrounded by discouraging people; the "why" will help me reach deep down into my core to find the strength I need to move forward towards my goals."

The "why" will instill within me
the foundation to sustain the
pursuit for the life that I want
to have, or that I want
to provide for others.

"That's right," replied Mr. W. "This is the step that many people skip over when they create their master plans to succeed. Yet it is the most important step. Without crystallizing in their plans the "why" for each goal, they are setting themselves up for inevitable frustration and failure. It is the foundation that needs to be established to overcome all negative forces that will try to take us off the path that we want to travel."

You now have a great understanding of the power of the "why", replied Mr. W. "You can now move on to the next strategy, which is visualization."

Mr. W. pulled out a business card and handed it to Jacob. The name on card was J.J. Spark.

"Give J.J. a call and let him know that Mr. W. sent you. He will talk to you about the power of visualization to stay motivated. He is a successful motivational speaker that has mastered the practice of creative visualization."

Jacob thanked Mr. W. and excitedly left to call J.J. Spark to see if he was able set up a meeting for the very next day.

Motivational Principle:

When you set a goal, you must establish "why" it is important for you to accomplish the goal. The "why" will define the purpose of your actions and it will fortify your commitment to attaining the goal.

Game Changers

▸▸ Have you dedicated time to write down your goals?

▸▸ Have you clearly defined the "Why" for each one of your goals?

▸▸ How will accomplishing each goal change or affect your life?

▸▸ What are the five things in your life that motivate you to succeed?

Fuel the Fire...Blaze Through Life

CREATIVE VISUALIZATION

*Whatever the mind of man
can conceive and believe,
it can achieve.*

–Napoleon Hill

J.J. Spark was not traveling on business. Jacob was able to set up a meeting with him the very next morning at J.J.'s office.

"Good morning J.J. Thank you for seeing me on such a short notice. I know that you are very busy."

"It's my pleasure. Mr. W. gave me a call and told me that it was important to meet with you. You are on a journey and I need to do whatever I can to help you along the way. Mr. W. did the same for me when I was starting my speaking career. He just asked one thing of me in repayment for the time that he invested with me."

"What was that?" asked Jacob.

"The principle of paying it forward," J.J. replied. "He had me promise that I would pass along the knowledge that he gave to me. Mr. W. believes that empowering people with the wisdom to pursue their dreams is the greatest gift that you can share."

J.J. continued, "I understand that you would like to learn about the second strategy that will help you fuel your motivation?"

"Yes, I learned about the power of the "why" from Mr. W. and he said that you have mastered visualization."

J.J. laughed, "That's very kind of Mr. W. I will be glad to share with you how to use visualization and why it will help you stay motivated."

J.J. jumped right into the lesson.

"Jacob, when you hear the word visualization. What comes to mind?"

"I see myself closing my eyes and thinking about what I want to achieve, why I want to be successful and how happy I would feel if I accomplished my goals."

J.J. asked, "What kind of details do you see when you are visualizing what you want to accomplish?"

"Details?", Jacob replied.

"Let me share a story with you", J.J. stated.

"When I first started my speaking business I faced many challenges, like many businesses in their infant years. Business was slow and the cash reserve I set up to carry me through the tough times was almost gone. I started to doubt my decision to be a professional speaker and my motivation was slowly disappearing."

J.J. shook his head while smiling, "Can you believe that? The motivator needed to be motivated!"

J.J. continued, "I was using visualization to keep me motivated, but not to its fullest extent. Thankfully, I met Mr. W. and he shared with me the power of creative visualization. Prior to learning from Mr. W. how to effectively use visualization, I was closing my eyes and thinking about what I want to achieve, why I want to be successful and how happy I would feel if I accomplished my goals. Does that sound familiar?"

Jacob and J.J. shared a laugh.

J.J. continued, "My visualization evolved to the following."

J.J. closed his eyes, lifted his head, smiled, took a deep breath and then he shared his vision.

"I pictured myself standing on a stage, with a great big smile, wearing a nice blue suit, confident and well prepared. I was in an outdoor stadium with a sea of people that looked like it never ended. The sky above me was a bright blue and there were cotton like clouds scattered throughout. I could see the bold colors of the clothes that the audience was wearing. The energy inside the stadium was radiant and a slight cool breeze whisked by me every now and then. I felt the breeze glide through my hair. I was taking deep breathes living in the moment. The air smelled fresh. I felt tremendous energy within. I was excited and happy to be doing what I love to do. I looked out over the crowd and saw smiling faces. I could hear them cheering me on. They were exhilarated about the message I was about to share with them. Music was playing in the background and the lights were brightly lit on the stage."

J.J. opened his eyes and his face was filled with enthusiasm. His energy was infectious.

"This image filled me with excitement and fueled my motivation. It helped me stay positive through the tough times. As a result, on a daily basis I followed my plan and my business came to life."

Jacob's eyes opened wide. "I understand. It's like seeing a picture in black and white or seeing a picture in color, filled with energy and life. The picture packed with color and detail is invigorating", said Jacob.

J.J. answered, "The details create a real connection between you and your goals. Details, such as where you are standing, what you are wearing, seeing yourself being confident, who you are with, what do you smell around you, how you are feeling, what is the temperature, are you inside or outside, what you are hearing and what colors do you see."

"I never thought about all of those details", said Jacob.

"The details create a real connection between you and your goals."

J.J. explained, "The power behind creative visualization is that it brings your images to life. It makes them real in your mind before they actually occur. When you add vivid details to your visualizations it will help you stay motivated and you will want to take action. As you run through your mind viewing all of the details, you will get excited. Your desire to convert your amazing images to reality will help you stay focused. The more attached that you get to your images, the stronger your internal drive to accomplish your goals will become. If you don't create vibrant images, they become distant, cold and uninteresting."

"The power behind creative visualization is that it brings your images to life. It makes them real in your mind before they actually occur."

"If the images feel like they are farther and farther away, and dull, the motivation starts to diminish", said Jacob.

J.J. continued, "That's right. One main reason people lose interest in pursuing their goals is because the internal connection to their goals disappears. The inevitable result is the loss of the driving force necessary to make changes and daily sacrifices to attain the goals that were set."

"In addition," J.J. explained, "setting aside regularly scheduled times to practice creative visualization will provide better results. It will help sustain your motivation. For example, the times that I have set are in the morning when I get out of bed and at night when I am going to sleep."

"That makes a lot of sense. The more often that I connect to my images, the stronger my emotional connection will become. This in turn will feed my motivation", Jacob replied.

"You will discover tremendous power once you believe that you are going to succeed and it is clear what success looks like for you. You will believe anything is possible" said J.J.

"You are now ready to learn about the third step to stay motivated. You will need to talk with Mr. W. and he will tell you who you need to talk to."

"Thank you J.J. for sharing your knowledge and experiences with me," said Jacob. As he left J.J's office J.J. handed him a copy of an Adidas' ad and told him to read it whenever he is facing challenges.

Adidas's ad:

"Impossible is just a big word thrown around by small men who find it easier to live the world they have been given, rather than to explore the power they have to change it. Impossible is not a fact. It is an opinion. Impossible is not a declaration. It is a dare. Impossible is potential. Impossible is temporary. Impossible is nothing."

Jacob called Mr. W. immediately after he left J.J.'s office.

Mr. W. asked Jacob, "What did you learn from J.J.?"

Jacob replied, "I learned how consistently using creative visualization will help me stay motivated."

"How so?" asked Mr. W.

Jacob explained, "The detailed images that I will visualize using this process will help me stay connected to my goals, bring them to life in my mind and it will keep me excited about accomplishing them."

"Well summarized. You are ready to meet the next person. You will now learn how the concept of association plays a vital role in helping you stay motivated", said Mr. W.

Mr. W. gave Jacob the contact information for Susan Love, an executive for one of the top marketing firms in Los Angeles, CA. Jacob called Susan immediately after he hung up with Mr. W..

Susan agreed to meet with him the next morning.

Motivational Principle:

Creative visualization needs to be vivid and rich with detail. More is better. All of the senses need to be engaged; touch, sight, sound, smell and taste. You must practice creative visualization often to keep your motivation at the highest level.

🏆 Game Changers

▸ How often are you going to utilize creative visualization?

▸ What motivates you about the images that you are creating in your mind?

▸ Are you in the moment in the image or are you looking at yourself from a distance?

▸ Who can you share your vision with?

"THE POWER OF ASSOCIATION"

I am not a product of my circumstances. I am a product of my decisions.

–Stephen Covey

Jacob arrived to Susan's office, as always, eager to learn.

The receptionist greeted Jacob with a warm smile.

She said, "Susan is expecting you. She is in the meeting room."

When Jacob walked into the meeting room Susan was reading an article on encouragement in the workplace.

"Good morning Mrs. Love," said Jacob.

"Good morning Jacob, please call me Susan."

"I am sorry to interrupt your reading."

Susan replied, "That's okay, I was expecting you. I was just finishing up my morning reading."

"Do you read every morning?" Jacob asked.

"Sometimes I read. Other times I watch a video or I listen to a CD or an audio book. My daily practice is to dedicate 30 minutes a day to self improvement. I read and listen to inspiring stories, self improvement books or magazines about my industry."

Susan continued, "When I was starting out in the marketing business, my mentor taught me to invest time in myself on a daily basis, to enhance my skills. He would tell me that the rise to the top would be painfully long if I only depended on the lessons I learned at work."

Susan smiled.

"I understand this is why you are visiting me today."

Jacob smiled and nodded his head.

"Mr. W. told me you would like to learn about the power of association and the role that it plays in helping people stay motivated?"

"Yes."

Susan asked, "When you think about the word association, what comes to mind?"

"My parents," stated Jacob. "Growing up my parents constantly reminded me to be cautious of the people I spent time with."

Susan agreed, "That's definitely a very important aspect of association. A well known motivational speaker, Jim Rohn, would say, "Don't hang out with the easy crowd; you won't grow."

Your progress in life will be hindered if you choose to associate with people who; are constantly complaining, who focus on problems rather than solutions, and who fail to take accountability by constantly blaming others for their problems. However, there is much more."

"Much more?" , Jacob's interest peaked.

He sat back, crossed his arms, and rested his chin on his hand as he listened intensely.

Susan expanded, "Association goes beyond the people you spend time with. It also relates to what you are constantly reading, watching and hearing. Think about the hours that we spend exploring the internet, watching television and movies; reading magazines and books; and listening to radio shows, music and audio recordings. All of these will have a profound impact on the way you think and act."

"I didn't look at it from that perspective," Jacob replied.

"Association goes beyond the people you spend time with. It also relates to what you are constantly reading, watching, and hearing."

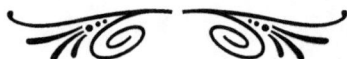

Susan explained, "Keeping a positive mindset to stay motivated is not always an easy task. Daily we are faced with many challenges that will take us on a roller coaster of emotions. This is why it's vital to surround ourselves with positive messages in relation to the internet, people, books, magazines, movies, music, and radio. If we allow negativity to enter our lives, we will succumb to the dooms day outlook that will drain our motivation. Time is our most important asset and we need to protect and invest it wisely."

"I'll tell you how I learned about the power of association," said Susan.

"When I first took a job in marketing my commute to my office was over an hour long. I would listen to talk shows about celebrity gossip, embellished news commentary about local and national problems and radio shows that did nothing but share negative opinions about others. I found all of these entertaining. However, I did not foresee how they were going to affect my daily motivation. I started becoming more judgmental towards others. My commentary about challenges focused on the negative. Also, my patience with those around me dwindled and I would get frustrated very easily. As a result, my work was suffering. My personal relationships seemed to have a lot more complications than before. Furthermore, my daily motivation to succeed was disappearing.

All in all, my life was not moving in the right direction."

Susan stopped talking for a brief moment and shook her head in disbelief.

Susan continued, "Then one day a good friend, that you know well, brought my behavior to my attention."

"Mr. W?", asked Jacob.

"Yes, thank goodness," Susan replied. "He had seen some changes in my attitude and he was concerned. He was more surprised actually, because it was not the Susan that he was used to seeing. Mr. W. and I had a long talk and we came to discover that what I was listening to for countless hours, was the cause of my negativity. I immediately changed my routine and started listening to audio books about positive communication, leadership and success. It took some time but my personal relationships and results at work changed for the better as the weeks passed. The end result, my motivation to excel had a brand new spark. Then as they say; the rest is history!"

Jacob and Susan both laughed.

Then Jacob shared his thoughts. "It is very clear to me now. We cannot expect to stay motivated all by ourselves. We need help to keep us focused and excited about pursuing our dreams and goals. Therefore, the people and things we associate with in our daily lives are the support system we need to help us along the way.

If we choose wisely with whom and what we associate with, we will surround ourselves with encouragement that will help us stay motivated."

Susan was pleased with Jacob's response, "That is a great explanation of the power of association. However, there is also one more piece that can be very difficult for some people."

Jacob ears perked up.

"The power of disassociation," said Susan.

"Disassociation?" replied Jacob.

"If we choose wisely with whom and what we associate with, we will surround ourselves with encouragement that will help us stay motivated."

Susan responded, "As you start to analyze where you spend your time, you will need to start disengaging with the things that do not create positivity in your life. The toughest part will be disassociating with negative people who have become a part of your life. This will be one of the most difficult decisions you will need to make. Unfortunately, this cannot be avoided. If you have people in your life that are toxic, you need to part ways. These people will act like an anchor, halting your progress and diffusing your motivation to excel in life."

"Wow. I can definitely see how that would be very tough for anyone," Jacob paused. "However, I do understand why it needs to be done. In order to stay motivated, positive encouragement is a necessity and these people are incapable of providing this key ingredient."

"This is an unfortunate reality," Susan responded.

They both sat silent in thought for a couple of seconds.

Susan continued, "We have to be cautious of everything that we allow to enter into our minds. Notice, I used the word "allow". We have control of whom and what we associate and disassociate with. We need to protect this freedom vigilantly and exercise its power daily to ensure our advancement in life."

"Too often we compromise our choices in order to please others." Jacob stated. "I see why we need to be firm in this area of our lives. We need to consciously protect our thoughts and feelings from negative forces. This will give us the strength to keep a positive mindset and to stay motivated."

"Well, I think that you have a clear comprehension of the power of association and how it will help you stay on course to achieve your goals. You are ready to move on to the next topic that will help you stay motivated. Call Mr. W. and he will tell you who you will need to contact."

"Thank you Susan for investing time in me", Jacob said sincerely.

"The only thing I ask in return is that you share this information with anyone that reaches out to you for guidance," said Susan.

"You have my word."

Jacob left Susan's office and called Mr. W.

Mr. W. was on his way to a speaking engagement when Jacob called.

"Hi Mr. W.", Jacob said, "I had a great meeting with Susan."

Mr. W. responded, "Great. What did you learn about association?"

"I learned that there is a lot more to the power of association than just with whom you spend time with. The things you read, watch and listen to on a daily basis have a direct affect on your motivation as well. Also, although it is a difficult task, knowing with whom and what to disassociate with is necessary."

"Well said," stated Mr. W. "The next person I will have you talk with will discuss a more private matter which will help you stay motivated. He will share some thoughts with you in regards to having faith. His name is Emmanuel Peace. He is a wealthy real estate investor."

Jacob called Emmanuel after hanging up with Mr. W. and he set an appointment to meet with him the following afternoon.

Motivational Principle:

You need to make a conscious choice of what you hear, read, see and with whom you spend time with. These will have a direct affect on your motivation.

Also, you need to make the decision to part ways with things and individuals in your life that are negative and impeding your progress.

🎯 Game Changers

▸▸ What are the positive things that you are going to start hearing, reading, and seeing?

▸▸ Who are the people that are encouraging and positive that you want to spend time with?

▸▸ What things are you allowing into your life on a daily basis that are negative influences?

▸▸ Who are the people in your life that you need to disassociate with?

"FAITH"

Ask and it will be given to you;
search, and you will find;
knock and the door will be
opened for you.

–Jesus

When Jacob arrived to Emmanuel's office the next morning Emmanuel was reviewing real estate contracts. Emmanuel heard Jacob come into his office and he went to the front to greet him.

"Welcome Jacob. It is a pleasure to meet you."

Jacob replied, "Good morning Mr. Peace. I appreciate you taking the time to meet with me this morning."

"Mr. Peace makes me sound much too old. I like to stay young at heart any way I can," laughed Emmanuel. "Please call me Emmanuel. Come on back to my office where we can talk without being interrupted."

Jacob and Emmanuel took a few minutes to get to know a little bit about each other.

Then Emmanuel said, "Mr. W. asked me to share my story with you. It is an example of how faith plays an important role in helping us stay motivated as we venture through our struggles in life. There is an old saying that goes;

If you walk up to anyone in the street and tell them, I heard about your problem. They will say, who told you?

The reality is that everyone has their own set of problems."

Emmanuel continued, "Jacob, there are two constants in life; change and challenges. Many times the changes will cause the challenges. Even though having a positive outlook is extremely important. We need to be keen to the fact that in our lives we will be faced with countless setbacks that will make it difficult to stay motivated. Even more so, there will be numerous instances when multiple challenges will arise at the same time and it will feel like everything is against us."

Jacob replied, "This has happened to me a few times and it is emotionally draining."

Emmanuel continued, "That's right. It drains your energy. Your motivation to pursue your goals fades away amidst the turmoil that surrounds your life. As a result, you go into survival mode. Your exuberance to excel in life is no longer a priority. Everything feels like it is out of control. Until...you turn to your faith."

Emmanuel smiled. "This is when faith will keep you grounded. It will bring you out of this downward spiral. It will give you inner strength and a sense of peace knowing that better times are ahead. Believing in a greater power, regardless of the religion, will create blessings in your life. You will find the inner strength to endure the tough times. Your perspective will change. You will start looking for the opportunities that lie within your challenges. Your motivation, though tested, will continue to resound within you to keep you moving towards your goals."

"Faith", Emmanuel continued, "reminds you to focus on the items that you can control, rather than trying to control the outcome of everything that is happening around you."

"Faith reminds you to focus on the items that you can control, rather than trying to control the outcome for everything that is happening around you."

"It is an overwhelming feeling when I make myself responsible for trying to find a solution for everything occurring around me. When I focus my energy and resources on the situations that I can change, I start seeing the results almost immediately," Jacob replied.

"You make a great point Jacob. This is a perfect time to tell you my experience," Emmanuel said.

"A few years ago, I went through one of the toughest challenges in my life."

Emmanuel paused. The old memories of what he endured were not easy to talk about, but he knew that sharing his story was important.

"During 2001-2007 life was treating me very well. The real estate industry was booming, I met a great girl, I was buying many investments and putting money in the bank. Then my world was flipped upside down within a 10 month period. In 2008 the real estate industry collapsed, I went through a divorce after being married for a few months, I was on the verge of losing the home I lived in, I lost almost every investment home that I purchased, my income dropped by 80%, I lost a substantial amount of money that I had invested in the stock market, my debt was piled high, I received a speeding ticket, then I lost my driver's license and I spent a night in jail due to a second speeding ticket for driving recklessly,"

Emmanuel paused.

"My life was in a downward spiral. I was angry, confused, depressed, and humiliated. I isolated myself from my friends and family that wanted to give me support, but I was too embarrassed to face them. Finally, after a few months of trying to ride this emotional roller coaster by myself I decided to surrender to my faith."

Emmanuel chuckled with a great big smile.

"I started reading the serenity prayer every day. What occurred after that was amazing."

Emmanuel recited the prayer to Jacob.

*"God grant me the serenity
to accept the things I cannot change;
courage to change the things I can;
and wisdom to know the difference."*

Emmanuel continued, "The day I decided to rely on my faith I felt the weight lifted off my shoulders. Previously I was focusing my efforts on trying to fix everything happening around me. Once I turned to my faith, I found peace in the fact that I no longer needed to spend time harping on the problems that were not in my control. Also, I was previously focusing on the problems, rather than on the solutions.

Once I narrowed the list of items that I needed to focus on to improve my immediate situation, things started improving for me."

Emmanuel continued, "I updated my resume and I found an opportunity that helped me continue on my career path, which allowed me to start paying down my debt. I made arrangements with the bank to keep my home. My ex-wife and I found a fair resolution to the marriage. Finally, I consulted with legal counsel to help me clear up my driving record. It was my faith that gave me inner strength and kept my spirits high throughout my rebuilding period. It was my faith that helped me stay motivated to continue on my path to success."

Jacob replied, "It is amazing the wonders that faith will perform in a person's life."

"Yes it is", stated Emmanuel. "My faith is my guiding light and I am very thankful for the blessings that I have today. My real estate business is generating outstanding revenue. I am debt free. I have a comfortable amount in my savings and retirement account. I married the woman of my dreams. I live in a spacious home that is in close proximity to my best friends, who are my parents. The issues with my driving record are a thing of the past. Finally, I have inner peace and I rely on my faith to guide me through the challenges that arise in my life."

Jacob felt the calmness in Emmanuel's voice.

Jacob responded, "It is very clear to me why faith must be an integral part of anyone's life. We cannot avoid the fact that life will bring us face to face with obstacles and we need to have a solid foundation bound in faith to carry us through. Thank you for telling me your story. I know that sharing your personal struggles is not an easy thing to do."

Emmanuel replied, "You're welcome. I am happy that you can learn from my experience. Without faith in a higher power, life is more difficult than it really needs to be. Lastly, I just want to warn you that there are many people out there that will want to push their religion on you. My advice is that you pray and reflect to allow your spirit to guide you. It may not be easy for you to choose how you want to pursue your spiritual life, especially if you have not made it a part of your life plan before.

However, at the end you will be extremely glad that you did. The reality is that long term success in life cannot be accomplished without the belief in a higher power."

"I completely agree", responded Jacob.

"Jacob, if you would like I can share one more story with you. It is one of my favorite stories about how you can choose to approach the problems that you will come across in life."

"That would be great," stated Jacob.

"The reality is that long term success in life cannot be accomplished without the belief in a higher power."

Emmanuel told his story.

"A young woman was complaining to her father about her problems and how difficult her life was. "Come with me", he said, "I want to show you something." He took her into the kitchen where he put three pots of water on the stove to heat. He cut up carrots for the first pot; he put two eggs in the second; and he put ground coffee in the third. After a few minutes he strained the carrots in the bowl; peeled the eggs and put them in another bowl, and into a cup he poured the strained coffee. The daughter said, "What's all this supposed to mean?" "Each of these items can teach us something about the way we handle adversity," the father answered. "The carrots started out hard, but the boiling water turned them mushy. The eggs went into the water fragile, but came out hard and rubbery.

The coffee on the other hand, changed the water into something better." The father continued, "sweet heart, you can choose how you will respond to problems. You can let them make you weak. You can let them make you hard. Or you can use them to create something beneficial. It's all up to you."

Jacob responded, "It reminds me of the quote;

10% of your success in life depends on what happens to you, and 90% of your success depends on how you react to what happens to you."

"You're right on target," responded Emmanuel. "You are ready to meet once again with Mr. W. He will discuss the last subject with you that is very important to staying motivated."

Jacob and Emmanuel concluded the meeting. Jacob called Mr. W. and he set up a meeting with him for the next morning.

Fuel the Fire...Blaze Through Life

Motivational Principle:

We are not in control of everything that occurs in our lives. Believing in a higher power that controls that which we do not control will bring us peace of mind. This will give you the freedom to exert your efforts in areas where you can make a positive impact.

Game Changers

- Do you try to control everything that occurs in your life?
- What role does faith play in your life?
- Who can you talk to about your faith?
- What are the blessings that you are thankful for in your life?

Fuel the Fire...Blaze Through Life

"COACHES AND MENTORS"

I've learned that people will forget what you said, people will forget what you did, but people will never forget how you made them feel.

–Maya Angelo

The following morning Jacob arrived at Mr. W's house. It was a beautiful sunny morning.

Mr. W. took Jacob to his favorite office, the backyard. They sat under a big red umbrella and shared a cold glass of iced tea.

Mr. W. took a deep breath to allow the energy of the day to whisk through his body.

He smiled, "One thing I remind myself to do every day is to be thankful for the blessings that I have around me. Make the most of every day," shared Mr. W. "The old adage to slow down and smell the roses is a great reminder to appreciate every step of your journey."

"As the great coach John Wooden said; 'The journey is the destination,'" Jacob said with a joyful tone.

Mr. W. and Jacob shared a soft chuckle as they both nodded in agreement.

"That is a perfect lead in to our last topic," stated Mr. W. "Having a coach or a mentor. All highly successful people have coaches and mentors. Elite athletes in all sports have multiple coaches. The president has an executive group of leaders that he meets with regularly for guidance. Famous actors have acting coaches that constantly fine tune their acting skills."

Mr. W. took a sip of his iced tea.

Mr. W. continued, "We have different ways to stay motivated. We need to know the "why" with each goal; we need to practice creative visualization; we need to be conscious of the power of association; and we need to rely on our faith, as Emmanuel Peace shared with you. However, there is one more piece to the puzzle. We also need someone that will hold us accountable with our progress. A person that can give us direction when needed, honest feedback, and that will infuse us with words of encouragement to keep us motivated. This is the role that a coach or a mentor plays."

"We also need someone that will hold us accountable with our progress. A person that can give us direction when needed, honest feedback, and that will infuse us with words of encouragement to keep us motivated. This is the role that a coach or a mentor plays."

"Do I need to find a professional life coach or mentor?" asked Jacob.

"That is a great question Jacob," Mr. W. replied. "It definitely can be if that is what you would like. However, it does not have to be a professional. Most importantly, it must be someone that has a proven track record of success. I advise you to be very cautious of whom you choose. Your mentor can be a top person in your company; a top person in your industry; a top person in another industry; a successful friend or family member; or a professional coach that specializes in the areas where you want to improve. If you happen to ask someone and they say no, do not let it discourage you. Keep looking for the right person that is willing to guide you along on your journey. Also, if you choose a person to be your mentor and then you realize that it was not the right choice, find another mentor. You and your mentor need to be on the same wave length in order for the relationship to be fruitful."

"How often do I need to meet or talk with this person?" asked Jacob.

"That will be determined by you and your mentor. At the beginning you may meet once a month. You may also decide to talk at least once a week or every couple weeks to discuss your progress. Then your meetings will be more spread out to give you time to put your activities into action. It will be important for you to set realistic time frames to measure progress."

Jacob replied, "The biggest reason people do not accomplish their goals is because of procrastination. I know that I am guilty of saying that I am going to start a new activity, and then I put it off. I see how a mentor will keep me from procrastinating with my activities because my mentor will hold me accountable."

Mr. W. moved his head up and down in agreement.

Mr. W. continued, "Also, the coach or mentor of your choosing will guide you throughout the process to make sure that you are focusing on the correct activities. Many times people will work hard but not smart. They work their tails off, while making little to no progress. If this happens too often, people get frustrated. Then eventually, people retract to their old habits which are comfortable."

"Also, the coach or mentor of your choosing will guide you throughout the process to make sure that you are focusing on the correct activities."

Jacob grimaced, "That has happened to me far too often."

Mr. W. shared his story. "When I was starting out in the motivational speaking business I was full of enthusiasm. I wrote a detailed plan to guide me to greatness as a speaker and I set lofty financial goals. I was confident that I was doing all the right things to stay motivated along the way. The "why" was very clear to me; I used creative visualization on a daily basis; I was cautious of the people and content that I associated with; and I was devout to my faith. My progress however, was dismal. I was at a loss and I was losing the motivation that I needed to build my business."

Mr. W. continued, "This is when I reached out to a very good friend of mine, a successful entrepreneur for over 20 years. His name was Allen Power. I met with him, explained my challenges and I asked him to be my mentor. We agreed to meet once a week at the beginning. Then we started meeting once a month. Today we meet once every two to three months. As a result, I was able to exponentially grow my business month over month. He encouraged me to stay on course when the business was tough. He gave me marketing ideas. He shared personal stories which gave me insight. He gave me honest feedback even if it wasn't what I wanted to hear. Most importantly, he held me accountable to the activities I set on my goals."

"Mr. Power helped you refine your plan, kept you focused and he fueled your motivation. It sounds like that made all the difference," Jacob stated.

"Yes," Mr. W. replied. "The right coach or mentor will make a tremendous impact on your progress. Let me finish this last topic with this quote about coaching. It summarizes what a great coach or mentor can do for you."

"I never cease to be amazed at the power of the coaching process to draw out the skills or talent that was previously hidden within an individual, and which invariably finds a way to solve a problem previously thought unsolvable."

—*John Russell*

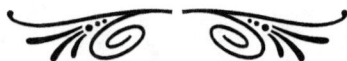

Motivational Principle:

A coach or a mentor will help you stay on plan. If you waiver or procrastinate on your activities, your coach or mentor will hold you accountable. This person will also give you words of encouragement to keep you motivated. We can never get too much positive encouragement along the way!

✦ Game Changers

▸▸ Who is your mentor?

▸▸ What are you looking for in a mentor?

▸▸ How do you react when you are held accountable?

▸▸ What kind of mentor are you for those that look up to you?

"Consistent Persistence"

I've missed more than 9000 shots in my career. I've lost almost 300 games. 26 times I've been trusted to take the game winning shot and missed. I've failed over and over and over again in my life. And that is why I succeed.

—Michael Jordan

Mr. W. was confident that Jacob was ready to start putting the principles he had learned into practice.

"As you have learned in the last few days," Mr. W. began, "staying motivated can be accomplished by anyone, but it will definitely take commitment. Each person's journey will be different, but similar. Though we all have unique lives, the obstacles that can affect our motivation have many similarities. I can't tell you that it will be easy to achieve your goals, but I can assure you that you have the same opportunity as anyone else to pursue them. Even though you will tumble many times along your path to success, jump right back up, dust yourself off and continue on your way."

Mr. W. took a serious tone.

He looked Jacob in his eyes and said, "The one thing you don't want to have in your life is the burden of regret for not pursuing your dreams. Pursue them tirelessly to live a life filled with adventure. Find ways to grow from every success and failure. Far too many people live in the should have, could have, would have circle of life. Make a decision today that, YOU WILL NOT BE THAT INDIVIDUAL."

This message resounded within Jacob and he stated boldly, "I will not be that individual!"

Mr. W. looked Jacob in the eyes and said, "That's right. Say it, believe it and live your life to the fullest every day."

Mr. W. paused slightly. "Jacob, I know that if you put into practice what you learned to stay motivated; you will succeed at the highest level."

Jacob glowed with eagerness.

"Thank you Mr. W. for sharing the 5 ways to stay motivated with me. I am excited to use what I have learned. I know that this will help me attain my goals in every aspect of my life. How can I repay you?"

Mr. W. replied, "You can repay me in only one way."

Jacob listened attentively.

"Make me a promise that you will pass this knowledge on to others."

"You can count on me Mr. W.", Jacob replied.

"Mr. W. Do you mind if I ask you one last question?" Jacob asked.

"Not at all," replied Mr. W.

"Would you be my mentor?"

"Are you sure I'm qualified?", replied Mr. W.

They both laughed.

Mr. W. replied, "It would be an honor."

Jacob now had a clear understanding of the 5 ways to stay motivated. He also had Mr. W. as a mentor.

The world was his for the taking!

He was ready to fuel the fire and blaze through life...!!!

"Consistent Persistence"

The End

Final Thoughts
from the Author

Mr. W. and the characters in this story refer repeatedly to the act of "paying it forward". I believe that one of your greatest gifts to others is to share with them the lessons in life that have helped you succeed.

Give the gift of knowledge without the expectation of anything in return and you will be showered with blessings.

As the world renowned motivational speaker, Jim Rohn, would say, "Help people get everything they want, and you will get everything you want."

God Bless!

Acknowledgements

I would like to thank my wonderful wife, Bianca, for inspiring me to write this book and for helping me with the layout. I love you.

Thank you to my amazing brothers, Fernie and Alex, for always being in my corner. I thank the Lord every day for blessing me with you.

Thank you to my dear friend Glenn for guiding me throughout the writing of this book. I appreciate your loyal friendship and thank you for being a great mentor throughout the years.

Finally, I want to thank my brother in law, Francisco, for taking the time to edit and proof read my writing.

About the author

John Arboleda was born in Quito, Ecuador. He made his journey to the United States with his parents and his brothers in 1981. He is an avid student of life. He received his Bachelor's Degree in Business Administration from the University of Redlands. He received his Masters Degree in Business Administration from California Lutheran University.

John has a passion for helping others discover their true motivation to succeed in life. He has been a motivational speaker and a sales coach since 1998. He hosted a successful radio show, The John Arboleda Show, which focused on self improvement.

Life is a beautiful journey and John loves sharing its daily blessings with everyone that he encounters.

Motivate And Inspire Others!

"Share This Book"

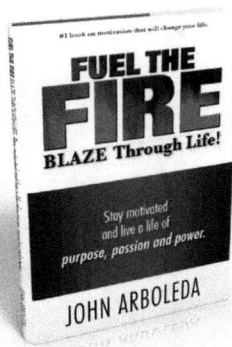

Retail $24.95

Special Quantity Discounts

5-20 Books	$23.95
21-99 Books	$22.95
100-499 Books	$21.95
500-999 Books	$20.95
1,000+ Books	$18.95

TO PLACE AN ORDER CONTACT:

arboledajohn1@gmail.com

Personal thoughts to stay motivated...

www.ingramcontent.com/pod-product-compliance
Lightning Source LLC
LaVergne TN
LVHW021515080426
835509LV00018B/2529